Baby Glen's VIVID IMAGINATIONS

Clay Bridges
PRESS

Shirley Jordan

Baby Glen's Vivid Imaginations
Copyright © 2023 by Shirley Jordan

Published by Clay Bridges Press in Houston, TX
www.ClayBridgesPress.com

All rights reserved. No part of this publication may be reproduced, stored in a retrieval system, or transmitted in any form by any means, electronic, mechanical, photocopy, recording, or otherwise, without the prior permission of the publisher, except as provided for by USA copyright law.

ISBN: 978-1-68488-098-0 (hardback)
ISBN: 978-1-68488-190-1 (paperback)
eISBN: 978-1-68488-099-7

Special Sales: Most Clay Bridges Press titles are available in special quantity discounts. Custom imprinting or excerpting can also be done to fit special needs. Contact Clay Bridges Press at Info@ ClayBridgesPress.com

Baby Glen's BACKYARD SAFARI

Shirley Jordan

Baby Glen, his friend Collin, and cousins Paris and Joshua were in the backyard planning a backyard safari.

Baby Glen pretended his backyard pool with his rubber duck, Ducky Danky, floating in it, was a small river with a large crocodile in it.

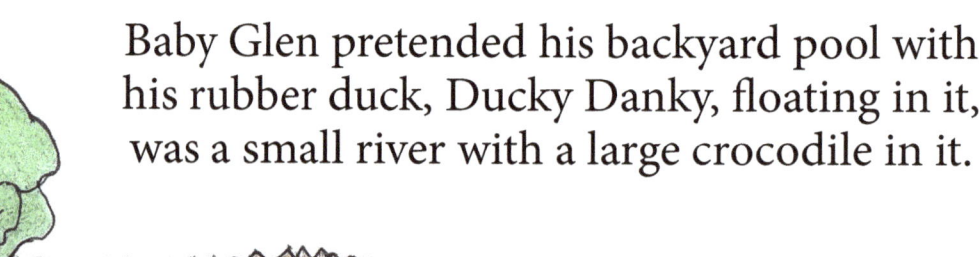

Paris saw a rope tied around a tree and pretended it was a snake.

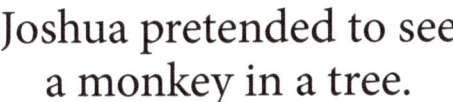

Joshua pretended to see a monkey in a tree.

Collin saw a dog in the backyard and pretended it was an elephant.

"All we are missing is a lion," said Baby Glen.

"Look," said Joshua.
"It's a cat on the fence.
Let's pretend it's a lion."

"Now we are ready to walk in the jungle," said Collin.

They all walked around the backyard holding sticks pretending the sticks were weapons to protect each other.

Just as Baby Glen went to jump into the
river to capture the crocodile,
his mother called him in for lunch.

All the kids ran
into the house.

They were ready
to eat.

"Wash your hands first," Mother said.
"You've been hunting for a long time, and
we don't want to bring germs to the table."

The kids all agreed not to bring germs to
the table for lunch.

"I'm first at the sink," called Baby Glen.

I'm second," yelled Paris.

"Third is for me," said Joshua.

I guess that makes me last!" cried Collin.

After everyone washed their hands, they rushed to the kitchen for ham sandwiches, chocolate chip cookies, and milk.

Being in the backyard pretending to be hunters made the kids tired. So after eating lunch, they went into the playroom to watch cartoons.

Later, Mother peeked into the playroom to check on the kids and found them asleep. She turned off the television and gave each one a kiss so they would have sweet dreams about Baby Glen's backyard safari.

Mother left the room silently so she wouldn't wake the tired hunters.

Baby Glen's
TRIP TO THE CITY

Shirley Jordan

Baby Glen's Great Aunt, Baby Ruth, wanted to take a trip to see the city. Mother was in the kitchen putting away the dishes. Aunt Baby Ruth asked Mother if she would take her for a ride in the car.

"Where would you like to start?" Mother asked.

Aunt Baby Ruth hadn't seen the city in such a long time. She didn't know where to start.

"I'm sure everything has changed," said Aunt Baby Ruth.

So she asked Mother to decide where they should start their road trip. Baby Glen was ready to ride. He didn't care where they were going. He just wanted to see the city.

"'Car rides always seem to put me to sleep," said Aunt Baby Ruth. "I hope I can stay awake long enough to see the changes the city has made."

"Oh, you will," replied Baby Glen. "There are a lot of nice things you will enjoy seeing."

"Are you ready?" asked Mother.

"Yes," replied Aunt Baby Ruth.

Baby Glen ran to the car.

"Come on, Aunt Baby Ruth!" he yelled.
"There is something I want you to see!"

"And what might that be?" asked Aunt Baby Ruth.

"You'll see when we get there," said Baby Glen.

Mother said that she thought she knew what Baby Glen wanted to show Aunt Baby Ruth.

Baby Glen sat in the back seat with Aunt Baby Ruth. He wanted to make sure she stayed awake for the long ride.

Mother drove slowly so both Aunt Baby Ruth and Baby Glen could see everything. Baby Glen didn't want Aunt Baby Ruth to miss his surprise.

Their first stop was at an amusement park.

"I don't remember this being here," said Aunt Baby Ruth.

Baby Glen watched as the kids drove the bumper cars.

"That looks like fun," he said.

Mother told Baby Glen that she would bring him back to the amusement park another time, but for now, they were showing Aunt Baby Ruth the city.

Baby Glen agreed with Mother. He wanted her to see his surprise stop before she fell asleep.

"Has downtown changed much?" asked Aunt Baby Ruth.

"Yes," Mother answered.
"You will be amazed at how different it looks downtown."

Baby Glen had never seen so many tall buildings. He asked Aunt Baby Ruth if the buildings could touch the sky.

"No," Aunt Baby Ruth answered.
"They're called skyscrapers because they look as tall as the sky."

"Wow," said Baby Glen as he looked up at the tall buildings with the sun in his eyes.

Mother said that she had an idea that's where Baby Glen wanted to take Aunt Baby Ruth. So, Mother took them around the neighborhood to see Baby Glen's school.

Baby Glen shouted, "There it is, Aunt Baby Ruth! There's my school over there! Can you see it?"

"Yes," Aunt Baby Ruth answered. "That is a nice school. It's a nice size also."

Mother agreed. She said she thought the school was large also.

Mother looked in the back seat at Aunt Baby Ruth, and she looked tired. Baby Glen saw Aunt Baby Ruth falling asleep, so he told Mother that it was time to go home. He said Aunt Baby Ruth had seen enough of the city for one day. So Baby Glen closed his eyes and pretended to be a taxi driver.

"Where to Ma'am?" he asked.

Then, he pretended to drive Aunt Baby Ruth home while she slept in the back seat of the taxi.

Baby Glen's BATH TIME

Shirley Jordan

It was time for baby Glen's bath.

He loved to bathe with his favorite toy, Ducky Danky.

Ducky Danky was given to Baby Glen by his great-grandmother, GiGi.

It was one of GiGi's favorite toys when she was a little girl.

Baby Glen loved going underwater with Ducky Danky.

Sometimes, he would close his eyes and pretend that he and Ducky Danky were at the beach.

Baby Glen enjoyed bath time. He didn't want to get out of the tub.

Mother had a special surprise for Baby Glen.

It was a new beach towel with a picture of Ducky Danky on it. Baby Glen was so excited.

He jumped out of the tub, grabbed Ducky Danky, and ran into Mother's arms.

He told Mother that it was his special towel and he wanted to use it every night.

Mother told Baby Glen she was happy he liked the towel, but he couldn't use it every night.

She dried Baby Glen off with his special towel and told him to get ready for bed.

Bath time was over, and Baby Glen was now ready for bed. So Mother took him to his room, put him into bed with his favorite teddy bear, Sleepy Snuggles, and kissed him good night.

Baby Glen thanked Mother again
for the towel and fell fast asleep.

Baby Glen's FIRST DAY OF SCHOOL

Shirley Jordan

It's Baby Glen's first day of school and he can't decide what to wear.

Mother suggested he wear his blue shirt with his blue shorts.

Baby Glen wanted to wear his red shirt with his blue jeans.

Baby Glen decided to close his eyes and turn around.

When he stopped and opened his eyes, he would make the choice for his first day of school clothes.

Baby Glen saw Myanh on his way to school. She lives on the same street two blocks down.

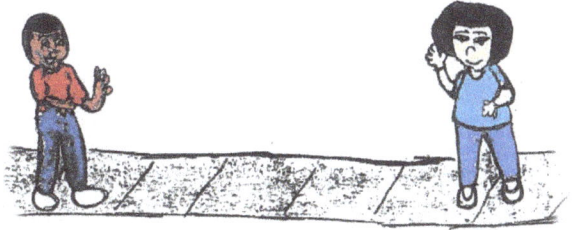

"Hi, Myanh," said Baby Glen.

"Hi, Baby Glen," Myanh replied.

Baby Glen asked,
"Would you like to walk with me to the bus stop?"

"Why sure," Myanh replied.

Baby Glen took Myanh by the hand and walked with her to the bus stop. Papa Glen and Mr. Lee, Myanh's father, walked behind them as they walked slowly in front of them.

As they walked toward the bus stop, Baby Glen told Myanh she looked very nice for the first day of school. The bus came, and everyone lined up to get on. The kids were pushing each other, trying to get on the bus.

The bus driver yelled, "No pushing!"

Then she said, "There are plenty of seats on the bus for everyone."

The bus driver told the kids to exit the bus one at a time without pushing one another when they arrived at their designated bus stop.

Finally, Baby Glen saw their school. The bus stopped, and the kids began to exit the bus. They didn't follow the bus driver's rules. They were pushing each other, trying to get off the bus.

"There is no need for pushing!" the bus driver yelled. "Everyone should exit the bus one at a time!"

Baby Glen and Myahn waited until the bus was empty before they tried to get off. They wanted to be safe for the first day of school.

While waiting on the bus for the other kids to exit, Baby Glen pretended he was a crossing guard. He pretended he was holding a stop sign and directing kids to school.

He yelled, "Come on, kids, you don't want to be late for your first day of school, do you?"

Baby Glen and Myanh were in the same classroom. Their teacher was a very nice man named Mr. Payne.

"Hello, Mr. Payne," said Baby Glen.

"My name is Glen, and this is my friend Myanh."

"Why hello," Mr. Payne replied.

Myanh saw two seats in the front of the classroom.

Myanh asked, "Would you like to sit by me, Baby?"

Baby Glen said, "It would be a pleasure to sit next to my best friend."

For recess, Myanh, Baby Glen, Joshua, and Paris took turns sliding and climbing while Collin played on the monkey bars behind them.

It was time for lunch, and Baby Glen had worked up an appetite.

He couldn't wait to see what was on the lunch menu.

The final bell had rung to end the first day of school. Finally, it was time to go home. The first day of school was over, and Baby Glen survived it.

He decided to stay a little longer after class so he could clean up around his area. He didn't have time to clean during school hours because he was too busy taking notes of the things he had learned that day.

Baby Glen told Mr. Payne that he wanted to stay a little later to clean up around his desk because it was the first day of school, and the kids were pushing people around to get on the bus. Mr. Payne said that it would be okay as long as Baby Glen didn't miss the school bus.

Myahn was waiting patiently outside for Baby Glen. She didn't want to walk to the bus stop alone. She knew the other kids would be pushing each other to get on the bus.

Baby Glen was finally finished with his cleaning, and he thanked Mr. Payne for letting him stay over a little longer.

Myahn and Baby Glen held hands as they walked to the bus stop. The bus driver was waiting for them. Baby Glen thanked the bus driver for waiting. Baby Glen knew he had a great first day of school, and he couldn't wait for the next day to do it again.

Baby Glen's HALLOWEEN

Shirley Jordan

It was the night before Halloween and all the kids were excited.

Baby Glen couldn't wait to put on his Spiderman costume.

Paris lived next door to Baby Glen, and she couldn't wait to put on her princess costume.

Myanh had a ghost costume, but she wanted to be a superhero.

Collin wanted to be a cat. So Baby Glen drew some whiskers on his face.

He wanted to see what Collin would look like as a cat for Halloween. The kids all laughed at Collin's whiskers.

"All we need now is a tail," said Baby Glen.

Joshua didn't like Halloween. He thought the costumes were scary. Baby Glen tried to get him to choose a nice costume.

He told Joshua, "All costumes aren't scary. You can choose a friendly costume for Halloween that isn't scary.

Collin said, "That's why I chose a cat. There's nothing scary about a cat."

Joshua didn't believe him.

"What about black cats? They are scary." Joshua cried.

"Black cats aren't scary," said Paris. "I have a black cat. His name is Fuzzy, and there's nothing scary about him."

"I saw a black cat in my backyard, and he didn't look scary to me," said Baby Glen. "He looked like he was hungry, so I gave him some milk."

What about the other kids that have scary costumes?" Joshua asked.

"It's all about fun," said Baby Glen. "All the kids just want to trick someone so they can get a treat."

"Yeah!" yelled Collin. "That's why it's called TRICK OR TREAT. You have to trick someone to get a treat."

Baby Glen said, "Dressing up in costumes means you are tricking other people. Some kid's costumes are scary, and some are friendly. But we all know it is other kids in costumes."

Collin said, "Most of the kids under the costumes are our friends, and there's nothing scary about them, right?"

The next day was Halloween. The kids couldn't wait for school to end so they could get ready for trick or treating. The teachers passed out some candy to the students at the end of the day. Most of the kids couldn't wait to get home so they could eat their Halloween treats they received from their teachers.

Some of the kids got dressed for Halloween right away. They had costumes that were superheroes, angels, and princesses.

After school, Paris spent most of her day at a pumpkin patch. She chose a nice pumpkin to take home to decorate for Halloween.

Later, Baby Glen saw Myanh and noticed she had on a different costume.

"I thought you were going to be a ghost for Halloween?" he asked.

"I know," said Myanh. "Mother brought home this angel outfit, and I liked it better. Besides, I didn't want to scare Joshua. He has enough to be worried about for Halloween. This will be his first Halloween with all of us, and I wanted him to see how much fun Halloween could be."

"Do you really think he will go trick or treating with us?" asked Baby Glen.

"Yes, I do," said Myanh. "Once Joshua sees us having fun. He will forget all about being afraid of scary costumes on Halloween."

Nighttime came, and there were lots of houses decorated for Halloween. Joshua was afraid at first, but when he saw the other kids getting candy, he decided to take a chance, too.

Kids were trick or treating everywhere. Baby Glen saw kids dressed as witches, superheroes, and pirates. He even saw Joshua dressed as a scarecrow enjoying Halloween night.

Baby Glen closed his eyes and pretended to see a witch flying on a broom, dropping candy to all the kids yelling, "Happy Halloween!"

The kid's bags were full of candy. Halloween was over. The kids were ready to go home and show their parents how much candy they got from trick or treating.

Their parents needed to check the candy to make sure the kids didn't get tricks instead of treats for Halloween.

Trick or Treat!

Baby Glen's SPECIAL CHRISTMAS

Shirley Jordan

It was the night before Christmas, and Papa Glen was in the room trying on his Santa costume.

Mother was threading her last string of popcorn.

GiGi was preparing a large box for Baby Glen's special surprise.

Mother was waiting for Baby Glen to come and wrap the string of popcorn around it.

GiGi asked Baby Glen if he wanted to help her wrap the last of her presents. She said she had a few presents left and could use Baby Glen's help.

Baby Glen agreed to help GiGi wrap the remaining presents. He said that wrapping presents would help take his mind off Santa.

Mother told Baby Glen to be patient. She said he didn't have much longer before they would bake cookies for Santa.

"This is going to be the best Christmas ever," said GiGi.

"Why the best?" asked Baby Glen.

"You'll see," said GiGi.
"Now pass me that box so we can finish wrapping the final gift."

Baby Glen passed GiGi the box. He saw two types of wrapping paper behind him.

"What about this wrapping paper?" he asked GiGi.

"Good choice, Baby Glen, you are such a good helper," said GiGi.

"I love Christmas time," said Baby Glen.

"Me too," GiGi replied.
"It's the time for families to share lots of love and joy."

GiGi and Baby Glen finished wrapping the presents.

"Let's go see if Mother finished stringing the popcorn," yelled Baby Glen.

"I think that is a good idea," GiGi replied.

Papa Glen was in the family room with Mother. They were putting the popcorn on the tree.

"Can I help?" asked Baby Glen

"Sure you can," said Papa Glen.

He lifted Baby Glen up high to reach the top of the tree. Baby Glen pretended he was in an airplane, going around and around in circles, putting strings of popcorn on the Christmas tree.

"Slow down, Baby Glen," yelled GiGi. "You don't want to have a crash landing while stringing the tree."

Mother brought out the cookies, and GiGi had a glass of milk.

"Is it time for Santa's snack?" asked Baby Glen.

"I'm afraid so," said Papa Glen
as he put a Christmas card on the table for Santa.

Baby Glen chose the position of the cookies and milk. He wanted to make sure Santa saw the cookies first.

He said, "If Santa sees the cookies,
he will eat them first and then drink the milk.
That way, Santa won't have a dry mouth
when he calls out to the reindeer."

It was time for bed. GiGi went upstairs with Baby Glen to put him to bed.

"No bedtime story?" Baby Glen asked.

"Of course, you get a bedtime story," replied GiGi.
"Now let's see," GiGi said. "What story should I tell you tonight?"

"What about a good Christmas story?" Baby Glen asked.

"I think I can handle that," GiGi said as she kissed
Baby Glen on the forehead.

GiGi chose a short Christmas story to tell Baby Glen as he fell fast asleep. GiGi knew Baby Glen was tired from all the activities he'd done earlier getting ready for Santa's visit. So when Baby Glen closed his eyes, he fell fast asleep.

"Sweet dreams," GiGi whispered as she tipped-toed downstairs, trying not to wake Baby Glen.

Glen wasn't the only one tired. Mother, Papa Glen, and GiGi were tired as well. Papa Glen ate the cookies and drank the milk that Baby Glen left on the table near the Christmas tree. Then his Mother and GiGi went upstairs to get ready for a special Christmas for Baby Glen.

Finally, it was Christmas Day. Baby Glen ran downstairs to the Christmas tree. There were more gifts than the night before. Baby Glen wasn't sure if he should wait for the others to come downstairs before opening one of his presents.

Then he heard a loud yell, "Merry Christmas!"

It was Mother, Papa Glen, and GiGi watching from behind the tree for Baby Glen to open his gifts.

Baby Glen noticed a large box under the tree.

He reached for the box, and it began to shake.

Baby Glen heard a strange sound coming from the box. He lifted off the top of the box and out jumped a puppy.

"A puppy," Baby Glen shouted. "You bought me a puppy!"

GiGi said, "I told you this was going to be a special Christmas."

"Yes you did," yelled Baby Glen, "and a special Christmas it is!"

"What will you name the puppy?" Papa Glen asked.

"I'm going to name him Brutus," said Baby Glen. "I always wanted a dog named Brutus."

"Merry Christmas," said GiGi.

"Merry Christmas," Baby Glen replied.

Baby Glen enjoyed having a puppy so much he forgot about his other presents under the Christmas tree.

"What about the other presents?" Mother asked. "Are you going to finish unwrapping your other presents?"

"Maybe later," Baby Glen replied. "I just want to play with Brutus for now."

Baby Glen said that Brutus needed to go outside to stretch his legs. He said Brutus was inside the box all night. He asked Papa Glen if they could take the puppy out for a walk.

Papa Glen told Baby Glen to help Mother and GiGi clean up the loose wrapping paper, and then they would take Brutus for a walk.

"Yes, Sir," yelled Baby Glen.

Baby Glen thought that this was the best Christmas ever. He rushed upstairs to put on clothes so that he could help GiGi and Mother clean up the mess that was made from opening up presents.

After helping Mother and GiGi clean up, he yelled, "We're done, Papa Glen! Can we take Brutus for a walk now?"

Papa Glen said, "Just a minute, son."

Then he gave Baby Glen one last present to open. It was a leash with a collar for Brutus.

"Now we are ready to go," said Papa Glen.

They put on their winter coats and took Brutus for a walk around the neighborhood to show off Baby Glen's Special Christmas gift.

"Merry Christmas, Baby Glen," said Papa Glen.

"Merry Christmas, Papa Glen," Baby Glen replied. "And what a special Christmas it is."

Baby Glen's
BED TIME

Shirley Jordan

Baby Glen spent the day with his great-grandmother, Gigi.

They had lots of fun together.
GiGi always had a story to tell Baby Glen.

Most of her stories were about Papa Glen. Baby Glen loved the stories GiGi told him about his father.

It was time for bed, and Baby Glen wanted a bedtime story.

"Tell me another story about Papa Glen, GiGi!"
Baby Glen cheered.

"Alright," replied GiGi,
"but you have to brush your teeth and get into bed first."

Baby Glen was so excited. He rushed into the bathroom, grabbed his toothbrush, and began brushing his teeth. He knew if he brushed too fast, GiGi would make him brush his teeth all over again, so he slowed down.

After brushing his teeth, Baby Glen jumped into bed.

"I'm ready, GiGi," he called.

"I'll be in shortly, Baby Glen," GiGi replied.

GiGi came into the room and sat at the side of the bed.

"I'm going to tell you a story about Papa Glen wanting to become a rock star," she said.

"A rock star?" asked Baby Glen.

"Yes, a rock star," replied GiGi.

Baby Glen's eyes lit up as GiGi began telling him the story about Papa Glen wanting to become a rock star.

GiGi said, "Your Papa Glen was a curious little boy who really loved playing the guitar."

He had always dreamed of being in a rock band. So, he and a couple of his friends from music school got together and formed a band. They would practice every weekend. Papa Glen wanted the band to be very good, so every weekend, the band would practice for as long as their parents would let them.

One summer, Papa Glen was ready to perform a concert with the band. So GiGi helped him set up a stage in her garage. The Band was excited to have a stage set up in the neighborhood around other kids that they all knew.

Papa Glen and the rest of the band passed out fliers to let their friends know about the upcoming concert. Everyone was excited. The band couldn't wait for the concert date to come.

It was going to be the best concert ever because everyone knew everyone. Finally, the time had come for Papa Glen and his rock band to perform. The front yard was full of kids from the neighborhood.

Everyone was friends and that made the concert even better.

The concert was a success.

It was the first concert in the neighborhood, and the kids talked about it for months.

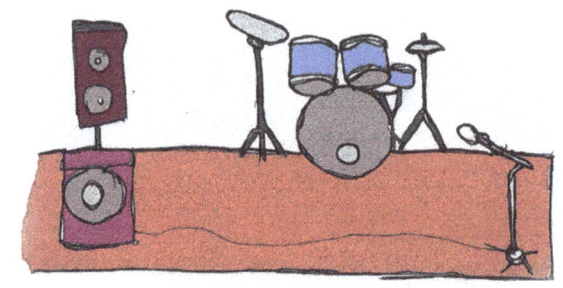

Baby Glen could just imagine Papa Glen singing on stage with his band. He just wished he could have been there.

So, Baby Glen closed his eyes and pretended he was watching Papa Glen singing at a live concert.

Just as the crowd began to cheer for Papa Glen, GiGi closed the book. It was the end of his bedtime story.

GiGi asked Baby Glen if he had any questions about Papa Glen wanting to become a rock star. Baby Glen had no questions, but he thought to himself how neat it was for GiGi to help Papa Glen complete his dream of becoming a rock star by creating a stage in her front yard for him.

GiGi gave Baby Glen a kiss on the forehead and told him to have sweet dreams as she turned off the bedroom light. Baby Glen closed his eyes and went fast asleep thinking about his bedtime story.

www.ingramcontent.com/pod-product-compliance
Lightning Source LLC
Chambersburg PA
CBHW050300090426
42735CB00027B/3500